UNLEASHING
THE POWER
WITHIN

A Journey of Self-Discovery Through Poetry

Lisa McCarthy

ISBN 979-8-89309-580-7 (Paperback)
ISBN 979-8-89309-582-1 (Hardcover)
ISBN 979-8-89309-581-4 (Digital)

Copyright © 2024 Lisa McCarthy
All rights reserved
First Edition

All rights reserved. No part of this publication may be reproduced, distributed, or transmitted in any form or by any means, including photocopying, recording, or other electronic or mechanical methods without the prior written permission of the publisher. For permission requests, solicit the publisher via the address below.

Covenant Books
11661 Hwy 707
Murrells Inlet, SC 29576
www.covenantbooks.com

Also by Lisa McCarthy

Inspiring Book of Poems, Dreams, and Stories

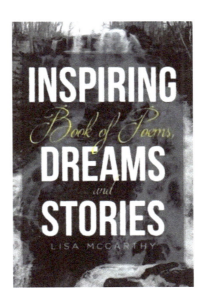

CONTENTS

Introduction ix

Breaking Free 1
New Year, New Chapter 2
The Power of Healthy Boundaries 3
Bloom 4
Boldly Free 5
Rediscovering Joy Through Our Inner Child 6
Freeing Our Mind 7
A Good Friend 8
Circle of Love 9
Dreams 10
The Real You 11
Warrior Soldier 12
I Am Enough 13
Embracing Life with Gratitude and Joy 14
Your Destiny Is Yours to Claim 15
Take a Chance and Move Forward 16
Seize the Day and Run Your Race 17
Say Yes to a Life of Fulfillment 18
The Butterfly's Lesson on Life 19
You Are More Than Capable 20
Happiness 21
Dance Through Life with Passion 22
My Name Is Destiny 23
You Are Extraordinary 24
We Are a River of Change 25
Life Is a Garden 26

Treasure Your Time..27
Stillness Within..28
The Lady Who Soared High 29
Love's Healing Touch 30
Unleash Your Imagination...31
Silence Your Mind...32
Listen to the Whispers of Your Heart 33
The Power Within...34
Eyes of a Thousand Dreams 35
Our Attitude Shapes Our World 36
A Helping Hand 37
A Single Gesture of Love and Unity 38
Promise Yourself..39
No Longer Bound by Negativity 40
A Beautiful Mind..41
The City of Gems 42
Living, Not Just Existing...43
Living with Purpose and Drive.. 44
Embracing Life's Wonders 45
Aging 46
Follow Your Intuition..47
Boldly Love Yourself..48
Stepping Out of the Shadows 49
Believe in Yourself 50
March On, Brave Soul...51
You Are a Miracle..52
What We Focus On 53
Hiking and Life 54
Walking Through the Red Cedar Trees 55
The Beauty of Nature..56
The Beauty of a Majestic Dawn 57
Golden Finches in the Rain...58
A Beautiful Day 59
Nature's Lullaby..60
The Beauty of the Gulf of Mexico's Sandy Beach 61
Walking Through the Lavender Fields 62

Fireflies at Night 63
A Wish upon a Star 64
My Words of Poetry 65
My Freedom Day 66
From Silence to Self-Acceptance 67
Hope for a Brighter Future Together 68
Peaceful Moments 69
This Is May 70
Summer Days 71
Remembering America's Independence Day 72
August Sunflowers 73
Thanksgiving Day 74
Christmas Night 75
Finding Self-Worth in God 76
Trusting God Through Life's Storms and Blessings 77
God's Masterpiece 78
Children of God 79
Open a New World as God Molds You 80
The Promise of My Heavenly Father 81
God's Love Shining Through the Rainbow 82
Blessed Love 83
Prayer for Guidance and Wisdom 84
When I Count My Blessings 85
On Wings of Faith and Grace 86
Ten Maidens 87
My Refuge and Saving Grace 88

INTRODUCTION

Dear readers,

Welcome to my second book, *Unleashing the Power Within: A Journey of Self-Discovery through Poetry*. This book aims to inspire and motivate you to find your inner strength and potential. Inside its pages, you will find many poems exploring different aspects of life, from discovering the power of healthy boundaries to rediscovering joy through our inner child and everything in between. Each poem has been carefully crafted to touch your heart, uplift your spirit, and encourage you to live life to the fullest. I hope that as you read through the pages of this book, you will be inspired to embrace your dreams and pursue them with passion and purpose. Whether facing challenges, seeking guidance, or simply looking for inspiration, this book has something for you. So sit back, relax, and let the words of these poems unleash the power within you. Allow them to inspire you to break free from your fears and doubts and embrace a life full of joy, hope, and fulfillment. Thank you for joining me on this journey of self-discovery and inspiration. I hope you enjoy reading this book as much as I enjoyed creating it.

Best regards,
Lisa McCarthy

BREAKING FREE

*T*his message is for those who fear the unknown, feel trapped and alone, believe they deserve misery, or that change is a fantasy. Those who love someone who has done them wrong think they can fix them with love alone. These thoughts flood the mind, locked away in torment, hiding bruises, scars, tears, and pain every day. But you are worthy of a life that brings harmony. Step out of bondage with faith and leap. I know it is scary, but the adventure is yours to keep. I will walk beside you, hand in hand, for I, too, once could not stand. But I believe in you, my dear. Leave the mess behind, and let God care for the rest. Your life will be full of love and happiness, so do not give up or lose hope. You are stronger than you know.

NEW YEAR, NEW CHAPTER

*A*s the new year begins,
A new chapter in life awaits, my friend.
Leave behind the past, negativity, and strife.
Embrace the future with hope and courage in life.

The year ahead is full of opportunities galore;
Seize them with determination, and strive for more.
Focus on growth and resilience,
And let go of all that causes hindrance.

Work on your mind and body; keep them healthy and strong,
For they are the key to achieving goals all along.
So welcome the new year with a happy heart,
And get ready to face life's challenges confidently; let's start!

THE POWER OF HEALTHY BOUNDARIES

Creating healthy boundaries is the key to unlocking your true potential. By recognizing your needs, values, and limitations, you can take control of your life and focus on your priorities. Healthy boundaries are essential for maintaining your emotional, physical, spiritual, and mental well-being. They breathe life into your soul, liberate your mind from negative thoughts, and enable you to pursue your dreams. Remember that you are worthy of respect, love, and kindness. Set healthy boundaries, and watch your life transform into joy, peace, and fulfillment. Let's unleash the power within us by creating healthy boundaries and taking control of our lives. We can improve the world by sharing our strength, courage, and compassion with those around us.

BLOOM

*B*loom beneath the ashes and dirt, forced to wait and live with hurt. Buried deep, I cannot see the light. Growth within is a constant fight. I will soon break from this state, bringing a beautiful new day to make. In the darkness, roots take hold, growing strong, both young and old. But light is needed to survive, blossom, and truly thrive. So as I lay in the dark so deep, a tiny sprout begins to creep. The freedom to bloom lies in our might, pushing through to reach the light. Deep roots grip the ground with unshakable strength. In the face of trouble, dare to keep the faith. Flourish like a flower under the sun or rain. With God's providence holding us, we can keep our faith and push forward, no matter how hard the journey may seem. So remember, no matter how buried you may feel, you have the power to bloom and flourish. You have the strength to overcome anything and everything that comes your way. Keep pushing, keep growing, and keep reaching for the light. Your journey may be challenging, but your spirit is unstoppable.

BOLDLY FREE

Set your sights high, aim for the stars, be molded through the challenges, and be healed from the scars. Believe in yourself and the power within. Persevere always, and you will win. With hard work and determination, soar and leave behind doubts and fears forevermore. No obstacle is too significant, and you will come alive. Know that you are capable of great things, and with every leap, your spirit sings. Respect the journey, learn from every strife, and grow stronger with each step of life. Stay true to your heart, let faith guide you, and watch your dreams come to life inside. Remember that greatness awaits—those who dare to chase their dreams with the courage to spare. So do not give up; be the best you can be, and in everything you do, be boldly free.

REDISCOVERING JOY THROUGH OUR INNER CHILD

As children, we were full of life, sparkle, and joy. We laughed and played without worries; our spirits were always high, pure, and brave. However, some people tried to change and shape us into who they thought we should be. Gradually, we lost sight of our identity, and our inner beauty began to fade away. Let's take a moment to reconnect with our inner child and rediscover the untamed spirit we once had. It's never too late to start anew and live joyfully like a child. Let's embrace our true selves and wear a smile, for every moment is worth it. Our spirits should soar, and our hearts should beat strongly as we journey through life and sing our song. Life is a gift, a precious treasure, and we should live it to the fullest in all its measure.

FREEING OUR MIND

*Y*ou have the key to freeing your mind from negative thoughts and attitudes. The power to break those chains in your mind is in your hands. This freedom lies within. Unlock your mind. Let it begin. Feeding negativity keeps us in bondage, where our minds cannot escape the prison we have allowed others and ourselves to create. Our minds are trapped; our hopes restrained. But the key is within our grasp. Unlock the door, break the clasp, and let it fall to the ground. Let our souls fly free by breaking those chains today and feeding on positivity. Feed your soul with love and grace. Escape the prison; leave no trace. Only you have this key to freeing your mind.

A GOOD FRIEND

A good friend is like your favorite song that never gets old. When sadness tries to invade, their light shines bright and never fades. When you hear your friend's voice, it brings happiness and healing. It is like a melody that soothes, inspires, and moves your soul. Finding a friendship like this is better than finding gold. They give you the joy to make you strong. Eternal comfort is never too long for when life plays a sorrowful song. They heal your soul with joy and peace. Their presence makes all worries cease. No matter the time or how far, their love is present, like a guiding star. It is a bond that is true and never ends. A treasure that is forever is a good friend.

CIRCLE OF LOVE

Surround yourself with friends who truly care.
Those who love you and are always there.
There is no judgment, just acceptance and trust,
Honest souls who treat you with respect.
In their presence, you feel safe and free,
A circle of love that will never bend.
These are the ones that will stay till the end.

DREAMS

*D*reams are a gateway to reality, a place where you can dance with glee. Everything you have made up become the truth as you unwind. Pursue your dreams with every breath. Believe in yourself until fulfilled; that is the quest. Never allow anyone to tell you it is impossible. Dreams are powerful and unstoppable. Dreams are a treasure worth fighting for; embrace them and soar forevermore.

THE REAL YOU

*B*e the real you. Are you trying to be something you are not?
Playing roles that are not yours is a complex plot.
Are you true to yourself or just trying to impress?
Do you fit in now or fake it to access?
A perpetual search for external resolution—
Is it worth it to keep up the illusion?
When inside my heart, I seek healing,
No time for complaints or concealing.
I will speak the truth and walk my path
Without fear of judgment or wrath.
Being trustworthy, I live a life free.
Being kind, I please the Almighty.
My heart is open, my spirit at peace.
I heal from within, and my love will not cease.
Be yourself, be real. It is the only way to feel.
Be the real you.

WARRIOR SOLDIER

*U*nbreakable, I stand tall and strong,
fighting for a life worth living long.
I endure all trials in my path with warrior courage and
steadfast faith. Survivor's hope and love, I hold dear.
Believing in myself, my heart is sincere.
Through hardships, I emerge bolder,
for nothing can destroy this warrior soldier.

I AM ENOUGH

I am enough every single day.
I am enough in every single way.
I will light the way for all to see.
Inspiring others, they, too, can be free.
No need to change, embrace who you are.
Each unique soul shines like a star.
Embrace your worth, let self-love grow.
Together, we will thrive, and confidence will flow.

EMBRACING LIFE WITH GRATITUDE AND JOY

I look up at the sky with my head held high and arms stretched out. I stand tall and sigh. The beauty of life surrounds me. At this moment, I feel free. The sun is shining bright above, a reminder to embrace this life with love. So I take a deep breath and embrace the day with gratitude and joy. Moments like this are rare and few, but they are precious reminders of what is true. That life is a gift to cherish and hold, a story yet to unfold. I will dance through life with courage and grace, knowing that every trial is just a test to ace. As I journey through each passing day, I will always make time to pray for the strength to carry on, the wisdom to make the right decisions, and gratitude for every blessing that comes my way.

YOUR DESTINY IS YOURS TO CLAIM

*R*ise, dear friend. Chase your goals without an end with every step. Throw off the weight, and reach for the stars without debate. There is a fire within your soul, a passion burning beyond control. So let it guide you to new heights and break free from doubts and frights. The journey may be challenging, but know that each obstacle will help you grow. And with the wind beneath your wings, you will soar above all earthly things. Never let anyone hold you back or make you feel like you are off track, for your destiny is yours to claim, and your success will bring you fame. So spread your wings, and take to the sky. Keep pushing forward, and do not say goodbye to the dreams that light up your soul and the endless possibilities they hold.

TAKE A CHANCE AND MOVE FORWARD

*T*ake a chance; move ahead.
Leave the past instead.
Embrace the journey, stay on track,
And never ever look back.
As you move forward, your bravery will grow,
And doubts will disappear the further you go.
Though uncertainty may cloud your view,
Trust in God; He will see you through.
Have confidence, and take a step forward,
Even if you cannot see what is onward.
God's guiding hand will lead you through the night.
His love will cast away any doubts in sight.
The path may be challenging; take that leap of faith.
Believe in miracles; they can happen.
With God by your side, you can succeed,
So do not give up; keep going and proceed.
Take a chance, move ahead,
And leave the past instead.

SEIZE THE DAY AND RUN YOUR RACE

*R*un your race with determination, power, courage, and strength, no matter the challenges. When obstacles try to knock you down, do not give up without a fight. Keep the unquenchable fire in your veins burning, driving you forward daily, breaking all chains, and conquering all that stands in your way. Remember, nothing can stop you from seizing the day.

SAY YES TO A LIFE OF FULFILLMENT

Say yes to a life that is fulfilling and real,
Where happiness and love you always feel.
Say yes to each sunrise; welcome each new day.
Appreciate all the good things that come your way.
Say yes to every minute; explore the world anew.
Let your soul be inspired; let your heart be true.
Say yes to a life that is wild and free,
Where truth and contentment will always be.

THE BUTTERFLY'S LESSON ON LIFE

*L*ife is precious; just ask the butterfly
That spreads out vibrant wings so fragile yet soaring high.
From the humble cocoon, transformation begins.
It perseveres through the storms and sunshine,
teaching us to cherish moments with sweet surprises.
Each delicate flutter is a reminder to be wise.
In its graceful flight, a lesson it imparts.
Appreciate the beauty in fragile, beating hearts.

YOU ARE MORE THAN CAPABLE

*I*n a world that often attempts to define your value, it may disregard and underestimate you. Nevertheless, it is important to recognize that you are more than capable. Despite being undervalued, your worth persists. And even when mistreated, you can emerge stronger than before. Embrace the struggles you face, and your path forward will come into focus. Remember always, my dear, that you are a person of worth, an unyielding force that cannot be stopped in all you do.

HAPPINESS

*H*appiness is like a dress
That flows freely without stress.
It twirls and spins, dancing in the breeze,
Bringing joy and putting hearts at ease.
With vibrant colors and endless grace,
It leaves a trace on every happy face.
A garment of warmth, woven with light,
Happiness radiates day and night.

DANCE THROUGH LIFE WITH PASSION

*L*ive passionately, dance freely, express your soul, and let your spirit flourish. With graceful movements, hearts shine bright, embracing all life offers. In harmony with joy, find your inner peace. Let the music guide you, your spirit soar. Dance through life, and create your destiny. Treasure every breath, embrace every opportunity, cherish happiness, overcome challenges, and make unforgettable memories. Breathe in love, release regrets, live fully, and leave a beautiful legacy behind.

MY NAME IS DESTINY

*M*y name is Destiny, and I sing in the darkness while chasing my dreams and wonders. I fearlessly embrace every opportunity and people around me, just like a child. My true calling and purpose in life motivate me to move forward. You may hear my small, still voice within you, so listen closely. I represent love, hope, and life itself.

YOU ARE EXTRAORDINARY

*R*emember, you deserve to be loved, respected, and fulfilled just as you are. Embrace your true self, and know you are worthy of acceptance and appreciation. Allow your unique qualities to shine, for you are extraordinary.

WE ARE A RIVER OF CHANGE

We are like a river, constantly changing and growing.

We break free to show our inner power flowing.

Our path to freedom and self-discovery leads us to victory as we gain new insights and unveil our identity.

As the day turns into night, we rise unbounded and shine brightly.

Our journey is full of twists and turns as we discover new paths and learn new lessons. We break free from limitations, shedding the chains that once bound us. Every day, we evolve and change, shifting our state of mind. Our journey of self-discovery is a path we must take as we uncover our true selves with every move we make.

So let us flow freely, like a river that roars, breaking free from our past and opening new doors. Let us transform with every passing moment, discovering who we are and embracing the bright journey ahead, like a beautiful star.

LIFE IS A GARDEN

*L*ife's garden flourishes with beauty and grace. It is a place of abundance filled with flowers, fruits, and vegetables. However, we must be mindful of the weeds that seek to choke what we have sown and smother our planted seeds. We can ensure a bountiful harvest by nurturing and watering each tender seed with care. Let us tend to our garden with love and attention, and watch it thrive as a testament to the joy and wonder of life.

TREASURE YOUR TIME

*T*ime is precious and short; do not let it waste away. Each second is lost, and we cannot replay. Value the moments, and make them count, for they do not last. Time is a river flowing fast. Time slips through like grains of sand, so cherish each heartbeat, every breath. Let it be your strength. Embrace today, for tomorrow is never a guaranteed day.

STILLNESS WITHIN

*M*ake time for yourself
To rest and find peace.
We are ever so busy.
In this life, we are in a rush.
But take a moment
To calm your mind and soul.
Find the stillness within,
And let yourself feel whole.

THE LADY WHO SOARED HIGH

There was a brave and bold lady, whose story was told in a world of wonders. She yearned to soar high, but reality denied her, leaving her dreams aside. She craved wings to fly in the sky, but her magical powers remained a dream. Though others soared above, she did not sigh. Hope whispered in her heart, "Someday, you will fly." One morning, she found delight as magical wings lifted her off the ground. No longer held back by earthly chains, she flew freely, with no bounds or pains. Finally, set free, a true inspiration for all to see. Her story of triumph and soaring high is a reminder that dreams can become real, so give it a try.

LOVE'S HEALING TOUCH

*L*ove's touch, so gentle, soft, and kind;
It mends the wounds that linger behind,
Healing hearts and soothing minds.
Through love's embrace, serenity we find.
An everlasting gift it brings
With hope and joy on angel's wings.

UNLEASH YOUR IMAGINATION

*L*et your imagination paint,
Vivid worlds in our minds,
Dreaming with eyes wide open
To create a place where anything can be.
Colors dance upon the canvas of thoughts,
Unleashing endless possibilities,
Where reality melds with fantasy,
A realm of wonder, where we are free.

SILENCE YOUR MIND

*S*ilence your mind, and find stillness within.
True peace will come, and calmness will begin.
Embrace serenity, like a waking dream,
And let your soul float down the gentle stream.
Balance your soul with each breath you take.
Feel the weight of worries break.
This silence is where true peace is found.
Leave fears and troubles behind on the ground.
Let worries drift away, like petals in the breeze,
And rediscover the joy in the depths of your mind with ease.

LISTEN TO THE WHISPERS OF YOUR HEART

*L*isten to the whispers of your heart. Follow its wisdom, and don't depart, for it will lead you to your destiny. Your heart will guide each step, both old and new. Please don't ignore it, for it knows the way through to the other side, where happiness and joy know no end.

THE POWER WITHIN

*F*ind the power that lies deep within,
Find the strength to rise again.
For you are stronger than you know,
Let your spirit grow and glow.
Believe in your heart; have faith in the keeper of your soul.
Embrace your worth, and make yourself whole.
With each step forward, let doubts go.
Break the chains that bind you so.
Unleash the fire that burns inside,
Embrace courage; let it be your guide.
Let your spirit soar high,
Unleashing the power that you hold inside.

EYES OF A THOUSAND DREAMS

*T*hese eyes shine like diamonds with mystery and grace. Even in the darkness, they reflect the stars and dance, casting pure light in a delicate trace. Their glimmer is captivating, love in disguise. The depths of a thousand dreams and secrets are hidden in those eyes. They whisper untold tales, a silent song, and hold the windows of a soul worth more than gold. In those eyes, dreams belong, where eternal beauty and miracles unfold.

OUR ATTITUDE SHAPES OUR WORLD

Our attitude is a decision that shapes every day,
Like a mirror, reflecting life in its unique way.
When we are grateful, we soar and conquer life's demands,
But bitterness can cause us to stumble in quicksand.
Let us choose kindness, empathy, and love above all,
And let our attitude paint our world with positivity, big and small.

A HELPING HAND

A helping hand gives love and understanding,
Showing compassion and never demanding.
It offers support and lifts the fallen.
With kindness and grace, it mends the broken.
A gesture of generosity, it freely bestows,
Bringing comfort and warmth wherever it goes.
In giving, we discover the joy that it brings,
In passing, we find the truest of blessings.

A SINGLE GESTURE OF LOVE AND UNITY

A single drop can begin a river's flow.
A single action can alter the status quo.
A single touch can form a bond between souls.
A single hope can guide you toward new goals.
A single love can endure the test of time,
Revealing the power of the divine.
In magnificence, grace, and merciful design,
We discover connection, purpose, and love so fine.
From the heavens, a gentle voice is heard,
Uniting us all in an unbreakable cord,
For in these fleeting moments, our spirits soar
Toward eternal bliss, where love endures.
In a world filled with chaos and despair,
A single gesture shows that someone cares,
Bringing peace and harmony everywhere.

PROMISE YOURSELF

*P*romise yourself today to live with intention.
Seek out joy, and never lose attention.
Promise yourself to hold onto hope,
To cherish beauty, and never let it go.
Promise yourself always to choose love,
To rise above hatred, reaching for the sky above.
Promise yourself never to give up the fight,
To embrace every challenge with all your might.

NO LONGER BOUND BY NEGATIVITY

*N*o longer will I let their words grow
Or allow their negativity to sow.
I won't stumble on their plans to trip me,
Instead, I will rise above, setting myself free.
It is a good day to stop caring what others say.
I know I am enough every day in my unique way.

A BEAUTIFUL MIND

A beautiful mind is fearless and bold,
Unafraid to challenge, to break the mold.
With each puzzle piece, it crafts its design.
With every challenge, it grows and shines.
Through logic and reason, it seeks the truth.
In the pursuit of knowledge, it finds its youth.
In the realm of curiosity, it roams free,
Exploring the depths of possibility endlessly.
With boundless imagination, it creates worlds unknown.

THE CITY OF GEMS

*I*n a city gleams a radiant treasure of gems so bright,
Sparkling like stars in the velvety night.
Amongst sapphires, emeralds, and rubies
are gemstones of dreams.
Opal streets shine, like a lover's warm embrace.
Amethyst echoes songs of grace.
A gemstone paradise beyond compare,
It is a vision so rich and rare.

LIVING, NOT JUST EXISTING

What does it mean to live and not just exist? Is living about listening to the whispers of a sun-kissed breeze and tasting the sweetness of love, like the fresh rain from spring? Or is it about pursuing our passions, hand in hand, and cherishing every breath we take? Living means more than just going through the motions; it's about finding beauty in everyday emotions. To truly live, we must embrace what we feel, laugh, create joy, and make existence persist. This is the essence of how to live and not just exist.

LIVING WITH PURPOSE AND DRIVE

I awaken with purpose, driven by desire. My eyes filled with determination; I soared higher. I conquer obstacles, persevering through setbacks. Courageous and strong, my spirit sings its song. I am motivated and unyielding to pursue my dreams passionately and give my best. With every step forward, I embrace my fate. In my heart, success surely awaits. I hold on tight through shadows and trials, knowing tomorrow will bring its light with smiles. For each path I choose, courage takes its place, fueling my dreams with determination and grace. With every step forward in faith, I conquer my doubt. Destiny is calling; I cannot live without it. My spirit soars high, with no limit or end, and I will always defend my goals and aspirations. We must live with purpose and drive, so I wake up each day ready to thrive.

EMBRACING LIFE'S WONDERS

What I live for is this precious life's embrace.
I am grateful for the blessings that cannot be erased,
Finding joy in each moment, shining so brightly.
Through the challenges I faced, I discovered my might
With each sunrise, a new day to explore,
Embracing the beauty this world has in store.
In laughter and love, my heart finds peace.
Each moment is cherished; life's wonders never cease.

AGING

*A*ging is a natural trend,
Fine lines and wrinkles we can find.
Memories cherished in old age,
Experience is worth more than wage.
Gray hair, wrinkled and wise,
Life's journey ends with a beautiful sunrise.
Though our youth may fade away,
Our wisdom shines brighter every day.

FOLLOW YOUR INTUITION

*T*rust your gut instinct; it knows what is best.
Your intuition is a compass, unlike the rest.
Others may advise and claim to know,
but you may need more than their advice to grow.
Deep within yourself resides knowledge, pure and true.
Listen to your inner voice; it will not mislead you.
Wisdom is what you truly need.
For your journey to succeed,
Trust your gut, and let it lead.

BOLDLY LOVE YOURSELF

*B*oldly love yourself and embrace your true worth. Find peace on earth, even in the midst of chaos. With every heartbeat, nurture your soul, let the healing begin, and make yourself whole. Remember that every struggle, flaw, and scar tell a unique story that makes you who you are. Forgive yourself for your mistakes as growth is the key to moving forward in life, happy and free. Empower your spirit, and let your light shine bright. Unleash your dreams, and let them soar high. In God, find your self-worth and strength. Stand tall and bold, forever loving yourself with all your imperfections, and watch your life transform in all directions.

STEPPING OUT OF THE SHADOWS

*S*tep out of the shadows.
Stop hiding your face.
Start showing the world what you are capable of with grace.
No more fears or holding back,
Boldly take back what is yours, and get back on track.
Embrace your power, and let your light shine.
Unleash your talents; reclaim what is rightfully thine.
Stand tall, be fierce, and let the world see
The strength and resilience that resides within thee.

BELIEVE IN YOURSELF

*B*elieve you are worthy of love's warm embrace,
And see the beauty and strength in every inch of your face.
Be open to receiving the tender kiss of love,
And nurture your inner beauty, like art from above.
You are deserving of immeasurable love and admiration,
A true treasure of divine creation.
Believe in yourself as a stunning sensation,
And let love guide you while your light shines without hesitation.
Remember, true beauty lies within your delicate heart,
So love yourself, and let your inner beauty be the start.

MARCH ON, BRAVE SOUL

*O*h, brave soul, keep marching on, for you are strong.
Break free from cords that held you for so long.
The past no longer binds. You are finally free,
With eyes wide open, a world you now see.
Embrace the change; let a new story unfold.
You are courageous, resilient, worth more than gold.
Keep moving forward; let your spirit soar high.
A new chapter awaits, darling; reach for the sky.

YOU ARE A MIRACLE

With every beat of your heart,
And with every breath you take,
Remember that you have a purpose.
You are not a mistake.
From the moment you are born,
You are a miracle, alive, and filled with wonder.
Your very presence radiates joy
And inspires others to chase their dreams,
No matter how big or small they may seem.
You are more than just flesh and bone.
You are a masterpiece from the very start,
Bringing hope and beauty to every heart.
Cherish every moment, and smile often,
No matter what life throws your way,
Because you make this world a better place every day.

WHAT WE FOCUS ON

What we focus on grows brighter each day.
Our mindsets may give rise to feelings that sway.
Be it love or fear, joy, or despair,
Our thoughts hold power and manifest like seeds in the air.
We must pick our focus with care and precision.
What we nurture will take on a life of its own decision.
Hope blooms like a flower, guiding us with its light,
And our thoughts, when tended, will shine ever so bright.
Our minds are like gardens, with thoughts as our seeds,
And with careful attention, we can plant what we need.
For what we focus on grows and takes shape,
So let's choose positive thoughts, and let negativity escape.

HIKING AND LIFE

A Tale of Perseverance

*H*iking can be compared to life; it is a challenging journey that tests our strength and determination. Even though we face obstacles, we keep moving forward and never give up because the rewards are well worth it. We may struggle with aching muscles and catching breaths, but we persevere, pushing through discomfort and stress. We climb hills and cross streams, determined to achieve our dreams. When we finally reach our destination, a feeling of joy and accomplishment washes over us, reminding us that we have overcome yet another obstacle. The spectacular view before us is why we set out on this journey, and the memories we create make the experience truly worthwhile. They inspire us to seek out new adventures and create new stories.

WALKING THROUGH THE RED CEDAR TREES

Oh, I love walking through the red cedar trees,
The aroma dances on the gentle breeze,
The branches are so full that birds chirp sweet melodies.
So high, peace fills the open sky,
In the forest, my spirit is set free,
and my heart is at ease.
Oh, I love walking through the red cedar trees.

THE BEAUTY OF NATURE

I love feeling the soft grass beneath my feet.

The sunshine kisses my face, oh so sweet.

Nature's magnificence is truly a sight to behold,

From sunsets painted with shades of gold

To blooming flowers, where secrets are waiting to unfold.

Nature's embrace brings joy, a calming peace that may seem simple, but they are complete,

With every step, my heart skips a beat.

The world is full of wonder and amazement, with endless opportunities to explore.

The small pleasures in life are what make it worth living for.

The birds sweetly sing as they soar through the sky.

These moments are what make us feel alive.

Let us appreciate all the beautiful things in life before we say goodbye.

THE BEAUTY OF A MAJESTIC DAWN

A beautiful sunrise of purple and pink swirls in the sky as the sun wakes up from its slumber; it happened so fast that I wished the moment would last even longer. My heart bursts into excitement at the lovely view, and all worries cease as I draw in another breath while welcoming the brand-new day.

GOLDEN FINCHES IN THE RAIN

Golden finches in the rain appear bright and bold, fluttering through clouds, a sight to behold. Their feathers shine, like drops on a leaf. With wings open wide, they catch my attention. Their colors are so pure and vibrant that I cannot ignore them. My heart does adore; their melodies in drops remain, golden finches in the rain.

A BEAUTIFUL DAY

*I*t is a sunny day. Birds soar in the sky,
Flowers bloom, and butterflies flutter by.
Nature's canvas paints a vibrant display.
The sun shines bright, a comforting ray,
Nature's symphony, a beautiful ballet.
Every moment is cherished, come what may.
Today is a gift, a beautiful day.

NATURE'S LULLABY

*N*ature's lullaby sets my soul free.
Rain dances on the trees so gracefully.
The wind blows whispers of melody.
Leaves sway and rustle tenderly,
Putting our hearts at ease, you see.
As night falls, stars twinkle and sparkle
In this peaceful symphony of dreams so gentle.

THE BEAUTY OF THE GULF OF MEXICO'S SANDY BEACH

Standing on the sandy beach of the Gulf of Mexico, I cannot help but admire the beautiful seashells scattered across the shore. The peaceful atmosphere, created by the gentle breeze and the swaying waves, puts me at ease and makes me aware of the natural rhythm of life. With each step, I sink into the soft, velvety, warm sand, feeling a sense of calmness. As I gaze out at the endless ocean, I am reminded of the vastness of the world beyond me, inspiring me to dream without limits.

WALKING THROUGH THE LAVENDER FIELDS

Walking through the lavender fields, surrounded by buzzing bees, we find peace and tranquility. The gentle sway of the soft purple petals beneath our feet and the fluttering of butterflies bring us joy and contentment. In this moment, time stands still, allowing us to cherish the beauty of nature and create memories that will last a lifetime, filling our hearts with happiness and warmth for years to come.

FIREFLIES AT NIGHT

*F*ireflies are a glowing wonder that catches my eye,
Twinkling sparks, a magical sight,
Guiding me through the blackened night.
They dance and flicker oh so brightly.
Their gentle glow always puts a smile on my face.

A WISH UPON A STAR

A wish upon a star, twinkling in the night,
Filling my heart with hope and pure delight.
Dreams take flight, guided by their radiant light,
Gently whispering secrets, enchanting and bright,
Granting desires, sprinkling stardust so right.
A wish upon a star lights my soul on fire,
Forever chasing dreams, soaring higher and higher.

MY WORDS OF POETRY

*M*y words flow like a river, pure and free,
a melody of thoughts that captivates me.
My pen dances across the page with glee,
painting vivid pictures for the world to see.
I find my voice and soul through poetry,
a sanctuary where my heart feels whole.

MY FREEDOM DAY

On June 17, 2010, I boarded a bus and left behind my toxic and chaotic past. I am grateful for the opportunity to start fresh and see things in a new light. Today, I celebrate my Freedom Day with gratitude for the courage it took to walk away. My life is beautiful and blessed, and I am grateful for taking that leap of faith. I have found my true home, surrounded by peace, and my soul is finally free. On this day, I give thanks to destiny for leading me to this place.

FROM SILENCE TO SELF-ACCEPTANCE

I used to feel like my voice was never heard. To protect my inner voice, I kept to myself and never said a word. I carried the heavy burden of pain and shame that should have never been mine to claim. I wished I could hide away from everything. But finally, I found the courage to release my voice and let it sing. Self-expression has helped me unveil everything that was hidden inside me. With every step I take, I walk a path that is my own. And with self-acceptance, I have indeed grown.

HOPE FOR A BRIGHTER FUTURE TOGETHER

*B*eing a source of hope for others is one of the most noble things a person can do. I aim to help people find their way through difficult times with kindness and understanding. I want to inspire everyone to find the courage to overcome their struggles and find peace. I strive to help people discover the power of hope and bravery and to work together to defeat the despair that can hold us back. Let us join hands and create a new story that leads us to a better future full of hope and possibility.

PEACEFUL MOMENTS

*P*eaceful moments, stress-free days,
sunny skies and uncomplicated ways,
and joyful laughter fill the air
with hopeful feelings everywhere.
Simple pleasures bring pure delight,
And heartfelt gratitude shining brightly.
Only good things are happening now.
Grateful for life and how
our worries and fears lay to rest,
living fully in each moment, feeling blessed.

THIS IS MAY

*T*oday is a good day. Yes, this is May. Where the flowers bloom, and trees finally have leaves, and nature sings its song. Everything comes alive for the first time since the cold caused everything to die and hibernate. May is the beginning of beautiful things to come. May awakens with its gentle breeze, breathing life into all creation. Flowers reach for the sky with joy and glee, smiling at the sun, grateful just to be. Butterflies stretch their wings and fly free with beauty for all to see and agree as they go by every flower, grass, around the ground, and sky. With the sun's rays, yes, this is May.

SUMMER DAYS

Summer is so lovely and hot.
It is like having hot coffee in your cup.
The sun is warming up you and me,
Up high in the sky, for all to see.
It makes us want to leave the house and have fun.
So off to the beach we run
For a swim and sink our toes in the sand.
The day is long, and the sun goes down at ten.
Oh, I love summer days.
It is filled with laughter, joy, and endless rays.
We soak up the heat and embrace the light,
for summer days are an absolute delight.

REMEMBERING AMERICA'S INDEPENDENCE DAY

*O*n this day of remembrance for our nation, we display our proud colors of red, white, and blue. The spectacular fireworks, lighting up the sky, fill us with wonder and gratitude. These symbols of freedom serve as a reminder of our country's strength. Together, we honor the courage and sacrifice of our heroes, who fought for our independence. May America continue to thrive and bring joy to our hearts every Fourth of July.

AUGUST SUNFLOWERS

Sunflowers in fields, August sunbeams. Petals reach high, a yellow-gold theme. Beneath clear skies, they turn and turn. Nature's crown, in elegance, they yearn. They are gleaming under rays so vast, a symbol of summer, a season that lasts. In the farming land, its beauty is untold—sunflowers in a field of gold.

THANKSGIVING DAY

On Thanksgiving Day, we gather around
With loved ones near, so joyous and sound.
Our hearts are complete, our spirits high,
As we give thanks and share pumpkin pie.
Around the table, a feast so grand,
With turkey, stuffing, and cranberry in hand.
We thank the Lord for all we have been given,
And cherish the memories we will keep living.
Forever grateful for this day of grace,
Our hearts are renewed in a warm embrace.
With blessings abundant and love so true,
We will cherish this day and all the year through.

CHRISTMAS NIGHT

Christmas night, a star so bright,
Shining down on this holy night.
Joyful carols fill the air
With tidings of love beyond compare.
In a humble stable, a precious birth,
Christ, our king, is finally here on earth.
To bring hope, peace, and salvation,
Let us celebrate this wondrous occasion.
Radiant joy fills our hearts anew,
Merry Christmas, dear friends, to each of you.

FINDING SELF-WORTH IN GOD

*I*t's common for many of us to feel undervalued and helpless while allowing others to underestimate our true worth. However, we must understand that we are worth so much more than that. Past experiences may have shaped our self-perception, but it is time to realize our true value. Our identity is found in God, and when we acknowledge our self-worth, beauty, and joy in Him, we can step into our destiny and fulfill our calling. We have a heavenly purpose and are called to do good works. No matter what has happened in our lives or our poor choices, God can still use us for His glory. We can be a light to the world. We are saved by grace as a gift, not because of our performance. God knows every detail about us; we are created in His image and are His children. We have royalty in our blood, and He knitted us in our mother's womb with a specific purpose. Sometimes, we may feel alone or fatherless, but our Heavenly Father loves us deeply. We don't need to seek validation from others because they will always disappoint us. True happiness can only be found in God; His light should shine through us. He will comfort us and wipe away our tears because we are His children, and He loves us beyond measure.

TRUSTING GOD THROUGH LIFE'S STORMS AND BLESSINGS

When life is rough, trust in God above.
Through trials and tribulations, find His love.
When life is smooth, give thanks with love,
Counting blessings, like stars in the sky above.
And when life seems to suck and blow,
Praise God, for He will help you grow.
For in the midst of the storms that come,
God's plan guides us towards where we belong.

GOD'S MASTERPIECE

I was created with such precision and care. It is truly remarkable. I feel grateful and humbled to be a unique and exceptional being, fashioned in God's image. I am part of His perfect plan, chosen from the start, and worthy of His love and grace. In His hands, I will always feel safe and protected. He sacrificed Himself for me on Calvary, and I will always belong to Him.

CHILDREN OF GOD

We are all children of God connected by love. His love is always there to restore us, even if we stumble and fall. Let us embrace each other with open hearts as sisters and brothers united in His grace. Every act of kindness we show each other reflects His love. Despite our differences, let us stand tall, knowing that love is the thread that unites us all together.

OPEN A NEW WORLD AS GOD MOLDS YOU

Open a new world, venture far and wide,
And get lost in the moments. Let your spirit guide you.
Turn the pages of life's book; embrace the unknown.
Feel free to enter where seeds of courage are sown.
Explore wonders of love, despair, growth, and more
As God molds you into someone you have never been before.

THE PROMISE OF MY HEAVENLY FATHER

*M*y dear child, I want you to have faith in your journey and trust that I have a plan for your growth. No matter what challenges you may face today, know that I will be there by your side, guiding you every step of the way. You can always count on me to care for you and never abandon you. Let my promise of peace of mind comfort you. I am your protector, your rock, and your shield. Keep your faith strong and your heart open, and we will shine brightly together. Remember, you are never alone, and with my love and grace, you will always find your way home whenever you feel unsure or lost. With love, your Heavenly Father.

GOD'S LOVE SHINING THROUGH THE RAINBOW

Whenever a rainbow appears in the sky,
It serves as a reminder of the promise God made up high.
It symbolizes love and kindness so pure
While bringing hope and blessings to help us endure.
Even during the storms and darkest clouds,
God's grace shines bright and should never be doubted.
His mercy and light set us free,
And a rainbow serves as His covenant, a guarantee.
God's love for us is unconditional and faithful,
and a rainbow's beauty reminds us of His promise,
    for which we are so grateful.

BLESSED LOVE

May our lives be filled with blessings,
Like rain from heaven above.
May our faith be strengthened
And our hearts be filled with endless love.
May your grace guide us through life's mysterious maze,
Shining light on all we do with unwavering grace.
May blessings continue to pour down, never ceasing,
Bringing everlasting joy and peace to our hearts, increasing.
May we always feel your presence
And know that you are near.
May we walk in your love and light
With nothing left to fear.
May we always trust in you
And never lose our way.
May we follow the path you've set
And never go astray.

PRAYER FOR GUIDANCE AND WISDOM

*D*ear God, please guide me through each day with your wisdom and light. May my thoughts be filled with understanding and insight into the mysteries of life, and may I learn valuable lessons along the way. Please grant me clarity and knowledge to guide my every step, and may the truth reveal itself to me with an open heart and mind, leading me toward the best path for me. I am thankful for your unconditional love and guidance.

WHEN I COUNT MY BLESSINGS

When I count my blessings, a smile spreads across my face.
My soul twirls with joy and dances with grace.
My heart beats with peace, and I'm filled with delight.
For all the things God has done, it's truly a sight.
My testimony is a gift that I love to share.
My voice rings with truth, and people stop and stare.
I sing songs of gratitude, and they soar up high,
Reaching far and wide, like a bird in the sky.
I'm grateful for every moment, and I remain rooted in love.
God's mercy and grace surround me like a dove.
So when I think of my blessings, I can't help but say,
"Thank You, Lord, for Your goodness every day."

ON WINGS OF FAITH AND GRACE

Dear Lord, I am grateful for the strength You have given me.
In a time when I was trapped deep in a well,
You reached down and rescued me.
You brought me to safety and helped me heal my wounds.
Your love has set me free,
and I am forever grateful.
Now I fly on the wings of faith and grace,
singing Your praises daily for guiding me along my journey.
Thank You for all that You have done for me.

TEN MAIDENS

The ten maidens stood with their lamps so bright,
Awaiting their king in the still of the night.
Their hearts are full of hope and anticipation
As they waited for their ultimate salvation.
But five were foolish and had no oil to spare.
Their lamps flickered and dimmed, causing despair.
They begged the wise for some to borrow,
But it was too late; their lamps hollow.
The king and the wise went on their way,
Leaving the foolish to face judgment day.
They learned a lesson they would never forget:
To always be prepared and never to regret.

MY REFUGE AND SAVING GRACE

*Y*our selfless acts and sacrifices have made me feel whole, washing away my sins and granting me eternal life for my soul. You are the source of my hope, strength, and inspiration, guiding me like a light in the darkness with Your compassion. I praise and honor Your holy name with every breath I take, for You have set me apart. I trust You entirely because You are always present and faithful. Your loving embrace brings me comfort, and in Your presence, I find grace. Your love and mercy flow endlessly like a mighty river, constantly replenishing and renewing my spirit. Your embrace is like a warm blanket that covers me, and in Your arms, I am free. My soul belongs to You, my Lord, and Your love restores me to my fullest potential. You are my refuge and saving grace, and I will always be Yours. As I stand here before You, my heart filled with love. I thank You for all You have done and who You are. Your greatness and kindness are beyond measure, and I am forever blessed to have You in my life.

ABOUT THE AUTHOR

Lisa McCarthy started writing poetry in seventh grade after she picked up a poem to read that reminded her of when she was four years old, picking raspberries outside, in her grandmother's garden, and how she just loved filling her bowl and her grandmother's bowl with those berries while leaving her raspberry bush bare and evidence all over her face. Reminded of the joy she once had before she moved out of her grandparents' house and into the toxic environment that brought her torment for years, she did not lose hope for the freedom she once had. Today, she lives a free life she loves and continues to move forward while encouraging everyone along the way.